Adventures of ELIJAH & LIAM

Elijah Takes 7

This book is dedicated to my Mom, Greta Thomas- my shero! Mom, thank you for always believing in me no matter what. Thank you for showing me that there is more in and to the world than the bubble people like to place us in; God's bubble is much bigger and impossible to pop!
You are such an inspiration- thank you for raising me.

Author Copyright © 2021 Tyesha Patterson
Illustrator Copyright © 2021 Nifty Illustration

All rights reserved. No part of this publication may be reproduced, distributed, or transmitted in any form without the permission of the copyright owner.

ISBN 978-0-5789-6872-8 (hardcover)

Written by Tyesha Patterson
tyesha.s.patterson@gmail.com

Illustrated by Nifty Illustration
www.niftyillustration.com
niftyillustration@mail.com

Welcome back!

If this is your first time reading the Adventures of Elijah and Liam, please note that this is the second book to the series; go check out Adventures of Elijah and Liam: Allow Us to Introduce Ourselves so that you are all caught up!

Adventures of Elijah and Liam is a series I decided to create during the pandemic to highlight how two young brothers were making the best of the global pandemic.

Personally, this has allowed me to follow a dream and passion of mine that is long overdue. I hope that you enjoy this adventure and remember to follow your dreams!

As the dust settles, Elijah quickly checks to ensure that Liam is ok; he finds Liam staring at a bright orange light. Elijah gazes and then explains to Liam that he is looking at the sun rise. He tells Liam that the sun is the largest star in the solar system and it brightens up the sky so that we can see part of the day without light.

Elijah takes a look around and is amazed at how big the safari is, a lot bigger than he imagined. He listens carefully to the sounds of the wind and then he hears a scary sound. "ROARRRRRR!"

Elijah suddenly jumps and scoops Liam up telling him that they must find cover as it is not safe for them anymore.

"ROARRRRR," this time the sound is much louder and closer than before. Elijah looks up and sees a very large shadow coming right toward them. Elijah immediately covers Liam and tells him to stay very quiet.

"AHHHH," Elijah screams as his Mom jumps out scaring them both. Elijah laughs, "Mom, I thought you were a lion because we crashed into a South African safari!"

"Yes, I know- I overheard you two and I could not help but to join in on the fun but I have something important to discuss with you and it is time for your brother's nap!"

Elijah joins his Mom in the family room in which she talks to him about his birthday. Each year, he always has a big party but this year will be different, his Mom explains due to social distancing.

Elijah's Mom tells him that this year, the guest list has to be small and that she feels it's best to include only his immediate family but promises that it will be fun.

Elijah reluctantly agrees as he is sad that he will not be able to celebrate his 7th birthday with friends whom he still misses so much.

"Happy 7th Birthday!" Elijah awakes to his Mom cleaning, lots of balloons, a kickboxing bouncy and more.

Soon, Elijah's closest family members arrive to celebrate him!

All day, Elijah enjoys a day filled with jumbo yard games, card games, water balloon fights, pizza, cake and ice-cream!

"Before you open your gifts and our guests leave, I have one more surprise for you that your uncle help make," states Elijah's Mom. She asks that everyone gathers in the family room and face the television. Next, Uncle PJ plays a video in which all of Elijah's close friends and family send him sweet messages to wish him a very Happy Birthday... The room shared lots of joy as Elijah's face lit up with excitement.

After photos, the guests leave and Elijah looks at his baby brother and says, "It's time for our next adventure to begin!" Elijah and Liam return to their helicopter and began repairs. Soon enough, they are able to hop in and begin their next travel. He looks over to Liam and says, "I am 7 now and there are 7 continents total with many countries to see; remember, we are now in the Motherland- the continent of Africa."

Liam coos at his brother and shakes his head with excitement, they then take off in their helicopter - eyes big, ready for what they will see next.

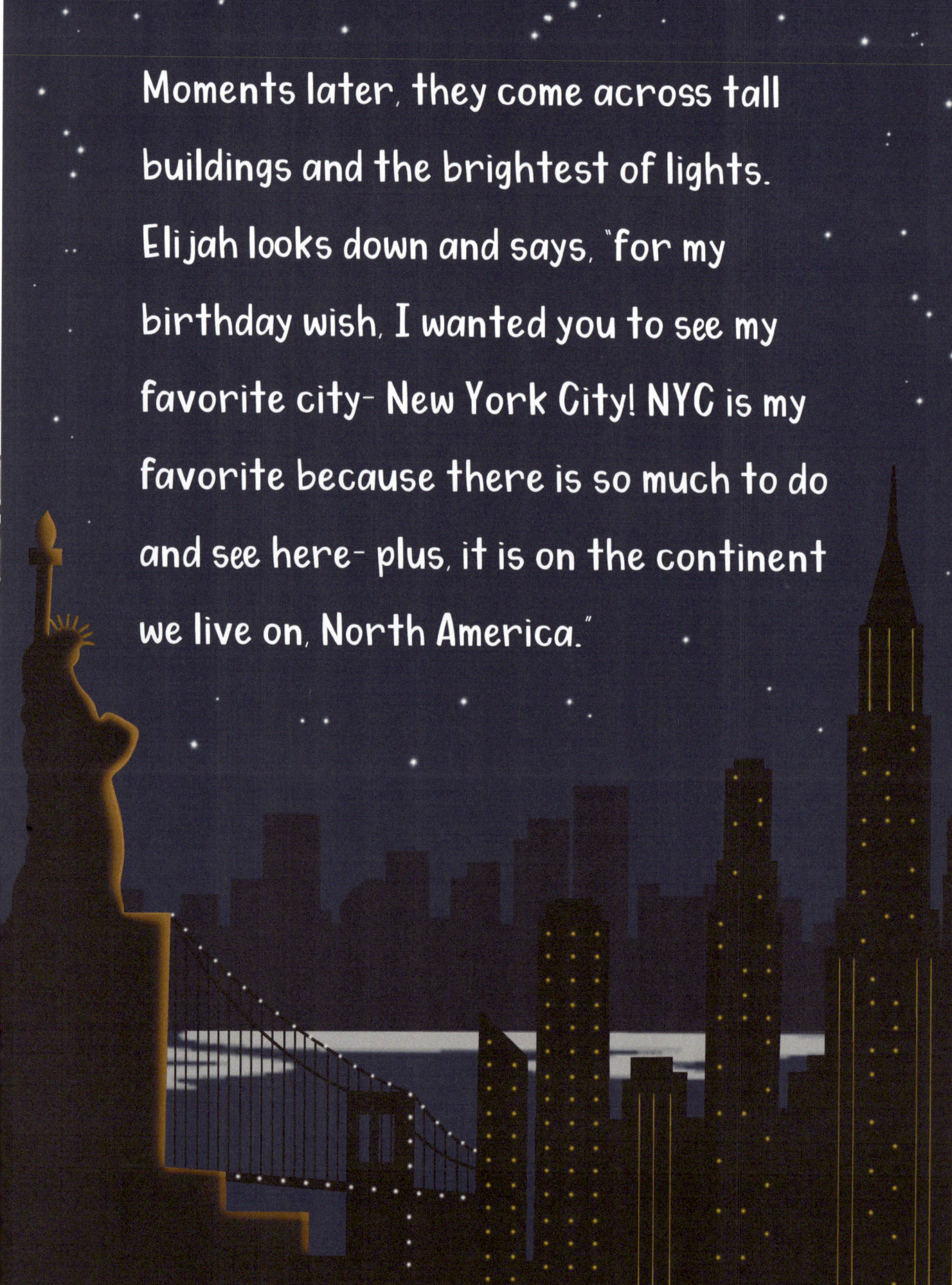

Moments later, they come across tall buildings and the brightest of lights. Elijah looks down and says, "for my birthday wish, I wanted you to see my favorite city- New York City! NYC is my favorite because there is so much to do and see here- plus, it is on the continent we live on, North America."

"Let's land and rest right here on top of the Empire State building so I can tell you more," Elijah exclaims as he balances on top of the kitchen table.

"Get down before you hurt yourself," Elijah's Mom yells from across the room; Elijah hops down and scoops Liam up and says, "we will have to continue this adventure next time!" Elijah and Liam then join their Mom in the family room to watch the news of the pandemic updates. Elijah is shocked to find that there is still no cure and more people are becoming sick daily. The news informs everyone that the safest thing to do is wear a mask when in public and to keep their distance.

Elijah is scared at first but then tells Liam, "Masks will only make our adventures that much more fun- watch and see!"

THE END

Stay tuned for what happens next!

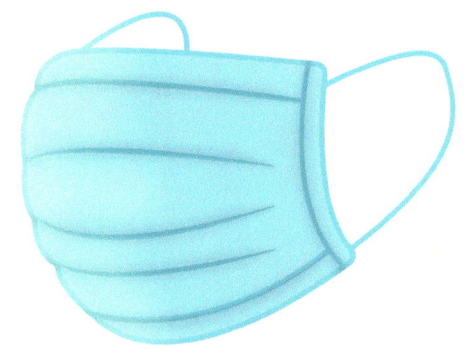

Meet The Author

Tyesha Patterson is a hardworking Mom that now resides in Easton, PA with her significant other and two boys! She has a passion for writing and looks to expand into other genres as she builds a legacy for Elijah and Liam. Tyesha will start a t-shirt line soon that will embody the meaning of Elijah Malachi and Liam Isaiah.

Tyesha can be reached by email at tyesha.s.patterson@gmail.com and found via social media on IG @tytalks_tyspeaks; @elijahandliam; and @ty_s_baby.
Thank you for your support.

Want to read about more adventures with Elijah and Liam?

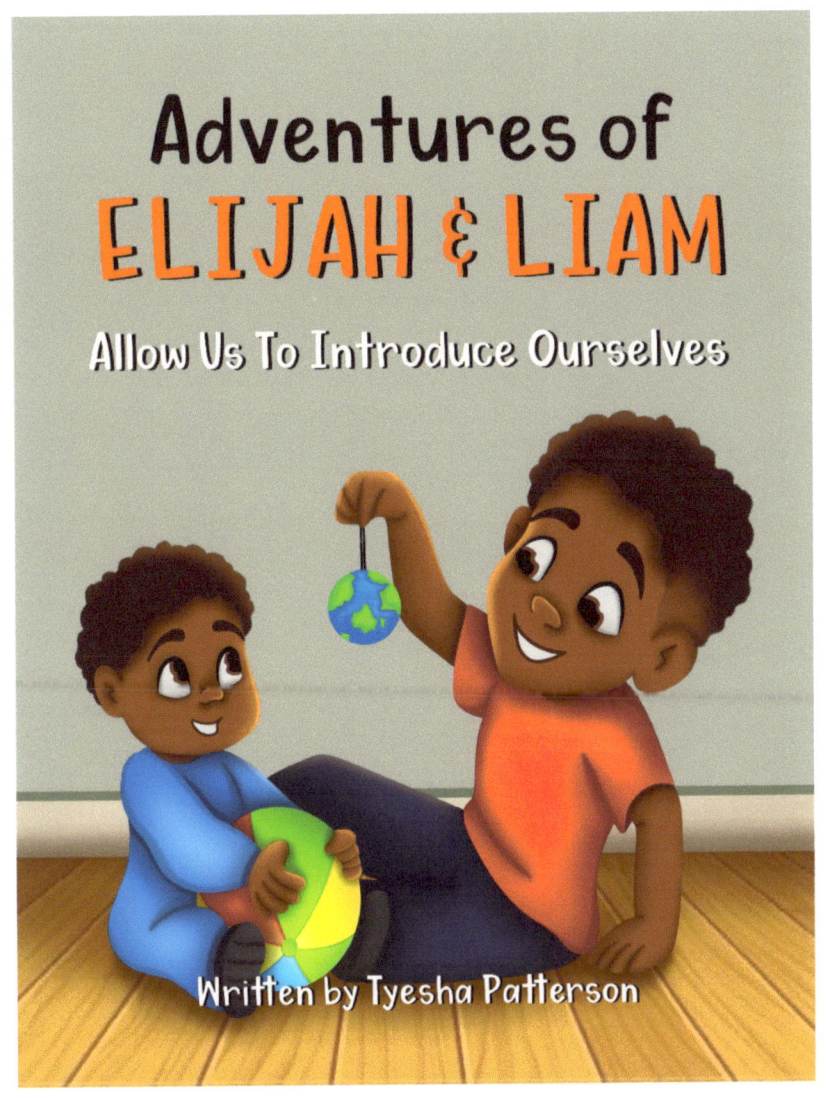

Book 1 is available to purchase now!

www.ingramcontent.com/pod-product-compliance
Lightning Source LLC
Chambersburg PA
CBHW040739150426

42811CB00064B/1789